YOU MUST BE J

Douglas Parker

You Must be Joking

Broadside

First published in Great Britain by Broadside in 1983

Copyright © Douglas Parker 1983.

This book is sold subject to the condition that it shall not, by way of trade or otherwise, be lent, re-sold, hired out or otherwise circulated without the publisher's prior consent in any form of binding or cover other than that in which it is published and without a similar condition including this condition being imposed on the subsequent purchaser.

ISBN 0 946757 00 3

Printed in Great Britain by
Cox and Wyman Limited,
Cardiff Road, Reading, Berks.

Set in Times New Roman by
JH Graphics Limited, Reading

Front cover design John Crane

Broadside
Studley House
68 Limes Road
Tettenhall, Wolverhampton

5

I've got one of those whistles that have a pitch which is so high it can only be heard by animals. I blew it the other day and was surrounded by an Alsatian, a Poodle and four Chelsea supporters.

A woman went to the doctors for some advice.

"There's something wrong with my husband, doctor, he never hears a word I say. What sort of complaint do you think it is?"

The doctor looked at her.

"That's not a complaint, love," he replied, "that's a gift!"

My mate has been visiting a Psychiatrist because he feels that people take advantage of him. He's feeling a lot happier now and has almost finished decorating the consulting rooms.

It might be said that marriage is like a self service cafe. You choose what you want, then when you see what your mate's got, you fancy some of that as well.

6

Don't you think it's a bit cruel that Dyslexia is so difficult to spell?

A fellow used to have a variety act with a parrot that did impressions. He even had a little fez for the parrot to wear when it did an amazing Tommy Cooper take-off.

Sadly, the novelty lost its public appeal and they couldn't get any bookings. Things got so bad that the chap had to eat the parrot to survive. Mind you, it tasted just like turkey . . . that bird could imitate anything.

"Just gone for a walk round the block."
   Anne Boleyn

When asked to explain the meaning of the word 'Bachelor' one school child wrote, 'A very happy man.'

"Where did you get that idea?" her teacher asked.

"My father helped me with my homework," she confessed.

7

If you can keep your head when those about you are losing theirs . . . perhaps you've misunderstood the situation.

A young man went to church for confession. "Oh father, I have sinned grievously. Women have been my downfall. On Monday it was a blonde, on Tuesday a redhead and on Wednesday a brunette."

"My child," replied the priest, "go home and squeeze the juice from a whole lemon and drink it."

"Oh father, will that purge me of my sin?" he asked.

"No child, but it will take the smile off your face."

Did you hear about the unlucky Northampton lady who advertised for a Sugar Daddy and was inundated with replies . . . from Lollipop men.

Sid: "When you quarrel with your wife, does she get hysterical?"

Stan: "Mine's worse than that, she gets historical."

8

Hear about the goalkeeper who was so unlucky that he saved a penalty . . . but let in the action replay.

"Mommy, why do fairy stories always start 'Once upon a time'?"

"They don't always. Your father's usually begin, 'Sorry I'm late, love, but I got delayed at the office'."

You know that your romantic life is dull when the light in your life is the one in the fridge.

Some hikers in Scotland were caught in a terrible snowstorm high up on a mountain. Fortunately, they found a small hut and were able to shelter. The following day a search party of Red Cross volunteers set out. For three days they trekked through the most hazardous conditions as the snow continued to fall. On the fourth day they came across the hut which was now almost covered by the thick snow. One of the party banged on the roof hoping for a sign of life.

"Who is it?" cried a feeble voice from within.

"The International Red Cross," came the reply.

"Well clear off," said the voice, "we've already given!"

9

The Department of Health have spent a considerable amount of time investigating the nutritional value of various foods. Their report indicates the main reason why children should eat green vegetables. If they don't they won't get any pudding.

Sid: "Every night my wife puts a mudpack on her face."
Stan: "Does it do any good?"
Sid: "It helps but I can still tell it's her."

There's a new deodorant on the market. It doesn't stop body odour but it makes you invisible and nobody can figure out where the smell is coming from.

A young golfer persuaded the club professional to play eighteen holes. When they had finished the round the young golfer enquired, "What do you think of my game?"

"Quite good," replied the Pro, "but I still prefer golf."

10

He's for the High Jump

An athlete won the hundred yards
And then he won the shot
The discus, mile and long jump
He won the bloomin' lot.
When asked by the reporters
How others he'd defeated
He said, "I train twelve hours a day!
And of course, I cheated!"

Wouldn't it be strange if Cliff Michelmore didn't really like going on holiday.

What a problem dress designers have. They not only have to make girls look slim, they also have to make men look round.

An elephant is a mouse drawn to government specifications.

11

The traffic is so bad these days that the government are bringing in new pelican crossing lights which read, "STOP", "GO" and "THREE TO ONE YOU DON'T MAKE IT".

Mind you, drivers don't help do they? My mate thinks defensive driving only applies if you own a tank. He's got three speeds in his car, fast, very fast and Hara Kiri. He's fastened a book underneath his car so that if he runs anybody over they've got something to read while they are waiting for the ambulance.

Hear about the civil servant who was admonished for being pleasant to a customer. He was excused when he explained that he was new to the job and had been startled when the client woke him up.

Nothing succeeds like a budgie.

12

One good turn gets most of the bedclothes.

A wife read her husband's fortune card from a weighing machine.
"It says, 'You have a magnetic personality. You are witty, intelligent and attractive...' it has got your weight wrong too!"

There's a new television set on the market with a feature you will really appreciate. It interferes with your neighbours electric drill.

A country lad went for a trip to the seaside and was watching the fishermen collect their baskets and nets.
"What are those things?" he asked.
"Lobster pots," came the reply.
"You'll never train them to sit on those things!" the lad retorted.

13

My mate brought a dictionary to read. He didn't think much of the story but said that he liked the way each word was explained as you went along.

A fellow staggered into Alcoholics Anonymous, fell over a chair and finished in a crumpled drunken heap.

"Oh dear," said the organiser, "when you turned up sober last time, you made me so happy."

"Well," burped the drunk, "today it's my turn to be happy."

A chap went to the Motor Show at the N.E.C. On the British Leyland stand was the chairman himself.

"Excuse me," says the visitor, "but I read in a magazine that you built a car in less than two minutes."

"As a matter of fact, sir," beamed the chairman, "we have built a car in one-minute twenty seconds."

The chap says, "I know . . . I've got it."

Nepotism can be relatively helpful.

14

A woman kept complaining to her husband that he never took her anywhere. So the next morning at 6.30 a.m. he gave her a nudge in bed and said, "How do you fancy coming to work with me?"

I knew it was going to be a strange flight when the Captain of the plane walked in with gold braid round his wellies. He apologised for the delay in take off. They were just putting the finishing touch to a patch in the canvas.

To be fair, there was plenty of in flight entertainment. We played 'spot the loose rivet' and the bingo was fun. The caller was a bit of a wag with cries of:

"All the fours, open the doors."

"Number three, we're in the sea."

Then there was the movie, of course. An interesting film it was too, 'Ghengis Khan meets Worzel Gummidge'.

*One chap, who was annoyed because he'd seen it before, forgot himself and, in a fit of pique, walked out. How well I remember that blood curdling scream as he plunged towards the ocean below. And the words of comfort from his fellow passengers, "Shut that *!*!/* door!"*

15

Young lady: "Should I wear my silk dress or my tweed suit."

Young man: "It makes no difference, I'll love you through thick and thin."

Hear about the sensitive rugby player?
He packed the game in because every time the other players went into a scrum he thought they were talking about him.

Lady complaining to her butcher. "That leg of lamb you sold me. I put it in the oven and it shrivelled up to half the size."

"That's strange," replied the butcher, "I bought a woolly jumper and when I washed it it shrank to half the size. It must have been off the same sheep!"

Two in every one people in this country are schizophrenic.

16

It is said that women worry about the future until they find a husband, whereas men never worry about the future until they acquire a wife.

A fellow went to the psychiatrist and said, "People say I'm mad because I like sausages."

"That's ridiculous," said the physician, "I like sausages."

"That's great," the fellow said, "you can see my collection. I've got thousands!"

Are nudists people who wear one button suits?

A pathetic little man was in the divorce courts accused of deserting his wife.

"And what have you to say to this charge?" he was asked.

"I wasn't a deserter," he replied, "I was a refugee!"

17

Public Inconvenience

'NOG was here' in '68 he scratched upon the door
I read the verses on the wall the censor never saw
And hear the chamber music,
water trickling down the wall
To flush the pipeways of the day
of man-made waterfalls.
How fragrant is the air in here
to those who've lost their smell.
So many people passing through
and passing out as well
But gratefully I'm sitting here
as one who contemplates
It's only fair, for after all,
I always pay my rates.

Criticism is something you can avoid . . .
by saying nothing
doing nothing
and being nothing.

18

A teacher in a small school in Ireland offered a pound to any child who could tell her the name of the most holy person in history. A solitary hand, that of a Jewish lad, was thrust into the air.

"It was Saint Patrick, miss," said Cohen.

"Correct," replied the teacher handing over the pound. "Now how is it that the only boy who knows the answer is Jewish?"

"Well, miss," piped up Cohen, "deep down I knew it was Moses . . . but business is business."

To err is human . . . but it feels divine.
Mae West

A small boy ate lots of cakes at teatime. He asked for another but his father advised, "If you have any more you will burst."

"Well give me another and stand clear!"

Always borrow from a pessimist . . . he doesn't expect to be paid back.

19

My pal's car is so unreliable he calls it flattery . . . because it gets him nowhere. Its previous owner was Coco the clown.

The Local Member of Parliament paid a visit to a Government training centre. He was impressed by the various skills on offer but paused with surprise at one room where a couple of hundred people were passing half a dozen pieces of paper to one another.

"One of our new courses," explained his guide. "This lot are training to be Civil Servants."

Just heard that the recession is so bad that even the people who don't pay have stopped buying.

And now a couple of words for hay fever sufferers, "Bless you!"

20

Full Marx

A mass of curly untamed hair
A hideous grin and vacant stare
Without a voice yet spoke so well
With movements that would cast a spell
And laughter, timeless, never worn
With mocking mime and honking horn.
Insane, yet somehow ringing true
You laughed at them while they at you
And heavenly notes your fingers stole
To reach beyond your outward role
Your battered hat and misfit suit
A talking face though always mute
And while the flicking picture gives
It's good to know that Harpo lives!

It is said that women like the simpler things in life . . . like men.

21

According to the medical profession, the first three minutes of life can be the most dangerous.

Mind you, the last three minutes are pretty dodgy too.

My uncle Humph was football mad and one day told his wife, "I'm just off to see the Wolves play in a cup-tie."

Wolves won and uncle Humph went off celebrating with his mates and, not surprisingly, drank one or two extra pints. At closing time being slightly the worse for wear, he was taken back to a pal's house and stayed overnight. On the Sunday morning he returned home and was greeted by his wife, "I thought you were going to see a cup tie?"

"I did but they had to play extra time," replied uncle Humph.

His wife without a change of expression said, "Well it will be your own fault if your tea is spoiled."

Amnesia rules . . . er . . . um.

22

Little boy went up to his aunt not long after she had arrived to stay for the weekend.

"When are you going to do your impression?" he enquired.

"And what impression is that?" she countered.

"Well," said the little boy, "Daddy says you can drink like a fish."

Have you ever thought . . .

That maybe the Joneses are trying to keep up with you.

That maybe gravity is a myth . . . the earth sucks.

That a specialist is someone brought in at the last minute to share the blame.

That the Inland Revenue is the country's most successful mail order business.

That embarrassment is watching someone do what you just told them was impossible to do.

If autopsy is a dying business, birth is a growth industry!

23

If you give your son a short first name it is important to give him a middle name also. Otherwise, what are you going to yell out of the door at him when you need to convince him that your patience is exhausted?

Maths teacher: "If I subtract 19 from 24, what's the difference?"

Little Johnny: "That's what I say, who cares?"

There was a posh lady who had a gardener whose one fault was that he didn't shave regularly. One day, in an effort to draw his attention to this, she said to him, "Tell me, William, how often ought one to shave?"

"Oh I don't know Ma'am," he replied, "you're not too bad, once a week should be enough."

Body building course testimonial: "Since taking your course I've become a real he-man . . . my husband is furious!"

24

The artist kissed his model tenderly.

"Do you know," he said, "you're the first model I've ever kissed."

"I don't believe it," she replied. "How many models have you painted?"

"Let me see," said the artist, "a vase of flowers and a bowl of fruit."

I used to use cliches all the time but now I avoid them like the plague.

A little boy was saying his prayers, "And please send some clothes for those poor ladies in Daddy's magazines."

When Arturo Toscanini was guest conductor at the Salzburg Festival, he feared that the Austrian Orchestra was no match for his flamboyant Italian temperament.

"Gentlemen," he grumbled at the first rehearsal, "the score demands 'con amore'. You are playing it like married men!"

25

Go to church on Sunday and avoid the Christmas rush.

They are having a competition on Brighton beach next summer. Kenny Everett will be buried in the sand and the first child to dig him out will get a thick ear.

Interviewer: "Are you good at typing?"
Secretary: "Not really but I can erase at seventy words a minute!"

Remember that as an employee you are totally dispensable . . . except that is when you want a day off.

Love is a many gendered thing.

26

A motorist was stopped by the police for a spot check.

"One of your rear lights isn't working," said the constable.

The chap got out, went to the back of the vehicle and kicked the bumper. The light came on immediately.

"That's very good," said the police officer. "You'd better go and kick the front and see if your tax comes up to date!"

Bad spellers of the world youknight.

One of the real tests of the recession. People are having to learn to do without all the things that their grandparents had never heard of.

A mate of mine has got a regular job at last. He changes the prices at petrol stations.

27

Only cannibals pick their relations.

A boy went into a toy shop.
 "How much is that little boat in the window?"
 Shopkeeper: "Eight pounds 40 pence."
 Boy: "That's expensive isn't it. I thought there was a sale on?"
 Shopkeeper: "No, it goes by a little battery inside."

My friend has a good head for money . . . there's a little slot in the top.

A man was examined by his doctor.
 "Now doctor, forget the fancy latin words. Just tell me in plain English what my problem is."
 "As far as I'm concerned," said the doctor, "you're just bone idle."
 "In that case," said the man, "give me the long Latin description so that I can tell the wife."

28

Do you know why women are said to drive more slowly than men?
Because they will do anything to stay under thirty.

Hear about the Liverpudlian who slept in his red and white scarf. Every night before he went to sleep he started whirring his football rattle and shouted, "Come on the 'Pool, come on the 'Pool."

After five years his wife couldn't stand it any more. "Sometimes I think you love Liverpool Football Club more than you love me."

He took one look at her in her curlers and face pack and said, "I love EVERTON more than I love you."

People who live in glass houses should beware of double-glazing salesmen.

29

A golfer went to confession.

"Father, I have to confess that I swore when I was playing golf."

"Tell me how it happened my son."

"Well, I sliced my tee shot badly and landed in heavy rough."

"So you swore?"

"No father, I played a superb second shot only to see my ball hit a divot and shoot into a bunker."

"So you swore?"

"No father, I took my sand iron and played beautifully onto the green to within a foot of the hole."

"You never missed the *!*!/* putt?"

Then there was the thick hoodlum who went to a drive-in movie. . . . He didn't like the film so he slashed the seats!

Remember that it is rarely the coldest girl that gets the mink coat.

30

He who hesitates . . . loses the parking spot.

A Birmingham man has just won an award. He managed to extract the name of the person he was speaking to at his local Social Security office.

Two small boys were chatting.
The first said, "I'm seven, how old are you?"
"I don't know," came the reply.
"Well do women worry you?"
"No."
"In that case I guess you're about four."

A fanatic is one who can't change his mind and won't change the subject.
　　　　Winston Churchill

31

I call my girlfriend 'Treasure'.
Well, I took her out one night and my mate said, "Good grief, where did you dig that up?"

Reply from a company asked to supply a character reference for a particular employee.
"Unfortunately we found that Mr Smith was something of a romancer. Even the wool he tried to pull over our eyes was half cotton."

Red Arrows flying display . . . if wet will be held in Town Hall.

You know you are getting old when you have that morning after feeling without having had the night before.

32

"Doctor, can I have some sleeping pills for the wife . . . she's woken up again."

Someone asked my uncle Humph, "Are you a native of Wolverhampton?"
"Certainly not, I was born here!" he replied.

It is said that the Mafia make you an offer you can't refuse.

The Glaswegian Mafia make you an offer you can't understand.

The Dublin Mafia make you an offer that they can't understand.

The Jewish Mafia, meanwhile, invite you to make them an offer.

A local chap has had his body tattooed all over with famous paintings. He has a Picasso on his chest, a Constable on his back and you should see the smile on the Mona Lisa when he sits down.

33

West Bromwich Albion are busy preparing for the F.A. Cup Final. They've all gone out to buy new television sets.

Let's be honest, the last time they won the cup, Dick Turpin held the coach up on the way home.

One of their strikers scored twice this week. First at a disco and then with a girl who works at Tesco's.

The trainer has put a bell in the ball so that the players can hear it coming.

They've found a major defect in the main stand at the ground . . . it's facing the pitch.

Is it true that Liz Taylor owns a drip-dry wedding dress?

They say that she's a marvellous housekeeper. Every time she gets a divorce she keeps the house!

'Watership Down' – You've read the book, You've seen the film . . . Now try the stew.

34

My Musical Background

I think it's fair to say that I come from a musical background. My grandfather was a gipsy violinist and in his will he left me an old violin and half a dozen clothes pegs. Working on the principle that you can't get much of a tune out of a clothes peg, my parents decided that I should have violin lessons. How well I remember those Saturday mornings dressed up in my leatherette helmet and leggings. With my violin case tucked under my arm I would stand on the front doorstep and pause to slap my thigh and shout, "Come on Tom only twenty miles to London." (Rather silly really since we had no cat and had always lived in the Midlands.)

Picture the scene. An Autumn vista, sunlight carelessly caressing the leaves as they lay like a carpet of crunchy cornflakes before my feet. (A useful interlude this. If you are getting bored with the story at least you can admire the scenery.)

I looked good, a smart young blade, and at eight years of age I reckoned I was pretty cool. My only flaw, I felt, was that I

35

had a broken lens in my spectacles and being from a poor family my father had boarded it up for the winter.

One particular Saturday morning is indelibly etched in my memory. As I walked along the street to my music class I noticed a kid called Bruce coming towards me. I knew it was him because I could just make out his giant frame as I peered through a knot hole in my spectacles. Bruce was an animal. A Neanderthal man. Although he was older than most kids in our area, he went to the Crippin Comprehensive, he was still waiting for his brain to arrive. His hobbies included stopping buses with his head and stealing hub caps from moving cars. When he was a few yards away he yelled, "Hey, Four eyes!"

I retained my cool and continued walking. Maybe I had misheard him.

He lifted one of his knuckles off the pavement and, pointing straight at me, yelled again, "Hey, Four eyes I'm speaking to *you*!"

That was it. My blood boiled. I realised

36

that the time had come to stand and be counted. I walked over to him and, pulling myself up to my full height I looked him straight in the kneecap. Caring little for his arrogance I addressed him with contempt.

"My name is Douglas Alphonse Montgomery Parker and if you wish to converse with me you must speak to me in the correct manner!"

I spent that winter in hospital with surgeons labouring to remove a violin. They said it was a good job I wasn't learning to play the flute.

I believe that Bruce is now doing very well in the diplomatic service.

It is actually true that my mother is tone deaf. The only tune she recognises is 'God Save The Queen' and she only knows that because everyone stands up.

37

One day at school Tommy was shown a picture of a deer. The teacher asked him if he knew what it was but Tommy could not remember.

"I'll give you a clue," said the teacher. "What does your mommy call your daddy?"

"Come off it," said Tommy, "you're not telling me that's a louse!"

Sid: "You got drunk last night and sold the Tower of London."
Stan: "So what's it to you?"
Sid: "I bought it!"

Insanity is hereditary – you get it from your children. One kid I know has sent so many adults barmy he gets a commission from the local psychiatrist and does a nice line in worry beads.

38

My mate reckons that if it's true that we learn from our mistakes . . . he must be getting a fantastic education.

Boy scout comes home crying.
 "I've been sent home for using my initiative."
 "How do you mean?" asked father.
 "Well they told me to pitch my tent," he replied.
 "There's wasn't any pitch so I used creosote."

My mate is very level headed.
He dribbles from both sides of his mouth at the same time.

Einstein rules relatively, OK.

A man visited Dudley and asked a local, "Does this town have any night life?"
 "Yes," came the reply, "but she's ill today."

39

Yosser Hughes went to see Quasimodo and said, "Gis a job."

Extra help was needed to ring the cathedral bells so he was taken on. The pair went up to the belfry and Quasimodo swung one of the giant bells towards Yosser who promptly gave it a 'Kirby kiss' – which is the almighty bang with the head for which he was renowned. Unfortunately, in doing so, Yosser lost his balance and went tumbling two hundred feet to the ground below. A crowd quickly gathered round the crumpled lifeless body.

"Who is it?" asked an onlooker.

"I'm not sure . . . but his face rings a bell," said another.

"I know him. He's a dead ringer for Quasimodo!"

Newspaper Advertisements

Bulldog for sale. Will eat anything. Very fond of children.

Mature lady, with dog, seeks post.

Young working girl seeks accommodation, must have bath, urgently.

40

Did you hear about the contortionist who went to the Social Security because he could no longer make ends meet.

The Lone Ranger and Tonto his faithfull companion were riding along when suddenly they were surrounded by Indians. A thousand Apaches on one side and two thousand Sioux on the other. There was an emotional tear in the Lone Ranger's eye as he turned to Tonto and said, "Well old friend, it looks like the end of the line for us."

Tonto paused, . . . then said – "Don't call me friend, you palefaced pig!"

When I was at school I used to think the teacher loved me because she put kisses against all my sums.

41

Remember the old days in France when they used the guillotine?

A chap was about to be executed when up dashed a messenger with a letter.

"Put it in the basket," said the condemned man, "I'll read it later."

The government has once again been accused of having too many ministries. This has been strongly denied in a statement issued by the Department of Hedgehog Fanciers.

Roget's Thesaurus rules OK, all right, very well, you bet.

There is a conference next week on Schizophrenia. You should go if you've half a mind to attend.

42

Little boy: "Grandfather, can you do an impression of a frog?"

Old man: "Yes of course, but why do you want me to?"

Little boy: "Because mummy says we won't have any money until you croak."

A fellow spent his entire life researching ghosts and was delighted when he finally found one which was friendly. He asked if he could photograph it and the ghost agreed. Unfortunately the flash bulb did not work. Which proves:

The spirit was willing but the flash was weak.

Out of the mouths of babes and sucklings

The party was in full swing when the host's small son tugged at his father's sleeve.

"Daddy," asked the puzzled child. "Haven't we had this party before?"

43

I told my girlfriend that she looked like a million dollars . . . all green and crinkly.

Mind you she was an ugly baby. She was so ugly when she was born the midwife slapped her mother.

She was so ugly that her mother fed her with a catapult.

If you look closely you can see the marks on her face where her mother missed with the frozen peas.

She's covered in bruises where people have been touching her with ten foot barge poles.

Archimedes rules . . . Eurekay!

A chap I know keeps a very intelligent dog. Remarkable animal it is.

I went round one evening and there was this dog playing cards with my pal.

"That's the most amazing thing I've ever seen," I said.

"Well he is clever," said my pal. "Trouble is that when he gets a good hand he keeps wagging his tail!"

44

A little boy asked his father, "How did I get here?"

His father said, "Well I put a seed in the garden and when I went out the following morning you had grown."

This impressed the little chap so much that he went out into the garden and planted a packet of seeds in the rockery. Early the next morning he went into the garden to investigate and there, sitting on a large rock, was a small frog.

"Well," said the litle boy, "I know you're ugly, but I love you . . . 'cos I'm your dad."

Hear about the gardener who was so lazy that he had his window box paved over.

Is a nudist colony a place where people go to air their differences and watch destiny shape their ends?

45

Introducing Mr Harold Smoothline

He glides like a man who's been oiled like a car
He nods for a drink while I wait at the bar
His smile never breaks as he talks through his nose
Quoting facets of news he relates them like prose
With monogrammed teeth and a hint of cologne
A sports job that purrs, he is never alone
With a girl on each arm you can see he feels proud
How I long for the day when he belches out loud!

How many times have you heard humans being compared to chimpanzees?
It is often true that the higher they climb the more they display their less attractive features.

Nostalgia is a thing of the past.

46

A small child had been allowed to stay up for her parents dinner party. Her mother, wishing to impress her guests, asked the youngster to say Grace. However, being nervous, the girl faltered but her mother prompted, "Say what daddy said before breakfast this morning . . . you remember, 'Oh God . . .'

To which the spontaneous response was, "Oh God, why do we have to have those awful people to dinner tonight?"

An apple a day keeps the doctor away but an onion a day keeps everyone away.

Literary girl: "What does he read?"

Religious girl: "What church does he attend?"

Society girl: "Who are his family?"

College girl: "Where is he?"

Definition of Well Informed.
Someone who agrees with your opinion.

47

Small boy boasting to his pal,
"I ran the hundred yards in five seconds."

"Don't be daft," said his pal, "that's less than the world record."

Thinking quickly the small boy countered, "Maybe so, but I know a short cut!"

Careers Officer: "What would you like to be when you leave school?"
Pupil: "A Lollipop man."
Careers Officer: "Why a Lollipop man?"
Pupil: "So that I won't have to start work until I'm sixty-five."

"The trouble with the world today is apathy."
"So what?"
"What's the difference between ignorance and apathy?"
"I don't know and I don't care."

Work for God. The pay may be poor but the fringe benefits are out of this world.

48

Humpty Dumpty sat on the wall
Humpty Dumpty had a great fall
All the King's horses
And all the King's men
Had scrambled egg for breakfast again.

A fellow arrived home from work and halfway through the evening his wife burst into tears.

"You never seem to notice me," she sobbed.

"But I do, my love," consoled the husband.

"Can't you see anything different about me today?" she asked.

"New dress?"

"No."

"New hairdo?"

"No."

"Come on then, what is it?" he conceded.

"I'm wearing a gas mask!"

Hear about the Civil Servant who failed the entrance exam? His feet fell off the desk.

49

It was the wedding anniversary of a couple who had been married for twenty years. The wife, a real battleaxe if ever there was one, thought it would be a good idea to celebrate with a meal at home.

"Why don't you catch one of the chickens and wring its neck?" she suggested.

"Seems hardly fair," her spouse replied, "to make a chicken suffer for something that happened twenty years ago."

Sign in a shop

God help those who help themselves.

It's tough to pay two pounds for a steak . . . but it's tougher when you pay one pound.

Did you hear about the short-sighted whale that fell in love with a submarine?
He followed it around the world and everytime the submarine ejected a torpedo the whale gave away cigars.

50

Two shipwrecked men on a desert island were bored so they decided to play a guessing game with film stars.

The first one started off, "I'm five feet three, with long black hair and sexy blue eyes. My measurements are 38-23-36 and I am suntanned and very appealing with luscious lips. Who am I?"

"I don't care who you are. Give us a kiss!" shouted the other.

A husband came home dead drunk and without his weekly pay.

"What did you spend it on?" his wife screamed.

"Bought something for the house," he mumbled.

'And what did you buy for the house?"

"Twelve rounds of drinks."

Mother: "Why are you standing in front of the mirror with your eyes closed?"

Tommy: "I want to see what I look like when I'm asleep."

51

What was that again?

The fund raising weekend camp has been organised to encourage young people to get together in healthy surroundings.

The local childrens home will benefit from their efforts.

In Brighton she was Bridget
She was Patsy up in Perth
In Cambridge she was Clarissa
The grandest girl on earth.
In Stafford she was Stella
The best of all the bunch
But down on his expense account
She was petrol, oil and lunch.

It isn't true that West Bromwich Albion have offered £60,000 for three Liverpool spectators.

52

I once met a chap who was fantastically rich. You know the sort, two Rolls Royce, and a Mercedes. He could even afford to travel by train without taking out a mortgage but he was frightened of bumping into Jimmy Savile.

Anyway, there I was, chatting away to him one day when he told me his story.

"When I first arrived in Wolverhampton," he said, "all I had were the clothes I stood up in, a pair of worn shoes with holes in and a stick over my shoulder with a blue cloth bundle on the end of it. Yet in less than a year I owned half the town and was a major shareholder in every industry that mattered."

"Amazing!" I said. "What a success story. Tell me, what was in the bundle you had over your shoulder?"

"Thirty-six million pounds," he replied.

Sid: "How come your car clock never runs down?"

Stan: "I always drive to work on a winding road!"

53

Remember, it's rude to whisper . . . but often a lot safer.

Talk about stupid. My mate said he could only boil an egg for two minutes because if he held them in the water any longer it burnt his fingers.

You know you are having a bad day when you enter a revolving door first and come out last.

Did you hear about the man who ran through a nudist camp with all his clothes on?
He was fined £50 for streaking.

54

A fellow meets his pal in the street.
"I'm just taking my wife to the doctors. I don't like the look of her."
"You'd better take mine as well," says his mate, "I can't stand the sight of her."

My girlfriend has a photographic mind.
It's a shame it never developed.
I call her Kodak because she's always snapping at me.

A fellow knocked on the door of a rather posh house.
"Do you believe in free speech?" he asked.
"Of course I do!" came the reply.
"In that case can I use your 'phone?"

Those who think they know it all upset those of us who do!

55

People who live in glass houses shouldn't.

British Rail have just announced a new plan to give the public a better chance of getting through to their 'Passenger timetable enquiries'. From the new year the number will be ex directory.

"What do you give a hare that's ill?"
"Hare Restorer!"

Don't count your chickens until they have been defrosted.

Do undertakers raise their prices to keep pace with the cost of living?

56

I've just received the following letter from my mother.

Dear Son,

Just a few lines to let you know how things are. You'll notice that I'm writing this letter slowly because I know that you can't read very quickly. You won't know the house when you come home. We've moved. We found the washing machine in the new house as soon as we moved in. I haven't quite got the hang of it yet. Yesterday I put six shirts into it, pulled the chain and we haven't seen the shirts since.

I went to see the doctor on Monday and your father came with me. The doctor put a small tube in my mouth and told me not to open it for ten minutes. Your father offered to buy it from him.

I've just heard that your sister had a baby this morning. I don't know whether it's a boy or girl so I can't tell you whether you're an aunt or an uncle.

57

Cousin Derek, you remember he worked in the distillery. He fell into a vat of whisky and drowned. Several of his workmates jumped in to save him but he managed to fight them off. He finally went under for the last time after three hours. They said he would have gone sooner but he had to get out four times to go to the toilet. When they fished him out his body was limp but they had to beat his liver to death with a stick. He was cremated on Friday and it took two days for the fire to go out.

Mind you, it's not all good news. Yesterday was so windy that one of the chickens laid the same egg six times.

Well I'd better close now because I'm going on one of those 'Mystery Trips'. It's usually a good night out. Last time they had a competition on the coach to guess where we were going. The first prize, a bottle of whisky, was won by the driver.

Until I see you,
your loving mother.

P.S. I was going to send you a fiver but unfortunately I've already sealed the envelope.

58

Hear about the salesman who said he'd got three orders in one day.
"Get out, Stay out, and don't come back!"

You know you are getting old when you are more interested in the food you eat than in the girl who serves it.

The parents of a little boy were worried because he didn't say a word until he was six years old. Then on his sixth birthday he turned to them and said, "I don't like this present you've bought me."

His parents were overcome with emotion.

"You can talk," cried his mother, "why haven't you ever said anything before?"

"Well," said the little boy, "everything has been okay up to now."

Is crazy paving all it's cracked up to be?

59

Hear about the thick cowboy who gave himself a hernia trying to hold up a stagecoach?

My mate is so thick he has to buy the TV Times to find out when News at Ten is on.

There's a fellow in Newcastle who reckons he has invented a game that in some respects is a bit like football.
Someone should tell him that West Bromwich Albion have been playing it for years.

Sid: "That bike I had pinched. The insurance company say they don't give me the money, they replace the bike with another one like it."

Stan: "That's fair isn't it?"

Sid: "For the bike, maybe, but I'm going to cancel the policy I've got on the wife."

60

Love flies out of the window . . . if the husband comes knocking the door.

There is an old schoolboy prank which you may recall. The trick was to take an empty sugar bag, fill it with soil and, after carefully resealing, place the bag in a public area. You could guarantee that the 'Sugar' would disappear in no time at all.

This childhood memory was brought back to me when the local refuse collectors went on strike.

Every week one of the locals wrapped his rubbish in gift paper and left it on the front seat of his car with the window wide open.

The parcel always vanished.

Did you hear about the chap who was such a puritan that he wouldn't speak to his wife because she was a married woman?

61

You know it's one of those days when you dunk a biscuit in your tea and half of it sinks to the bottom of the cup.

The mighty lion pounded through the jungle. When he met a tiger he stopped and demanded, "Who is the king of the jungle?"

"You are, Mr Lion." replied the tiger.

A little further on the lion met a fierce panther. "Who is the king of the jungle?" asked the lion.

"You are, Mr Lion," said the panther meekly.

The proud lion carried on walking until he met an enormous bull elephant. "Who is the king of the jungle?" demanded the lion.

Turning fiercely the elephant picked up the lion with his trunk and smashed him against a tree. Then he started kicking the lion around the clearing.

"Hang on," cried the lion, "there's no need to get upset just because you don't know the answer."

My neighbours are so posh that they water their potted plants with perrier water.

62

Church Notice

"As the cost of churchyard maintenance is so high it would be appreciated if those who are able would cut the grass around their own graves."

A large white stallion walked into a pub and ordered a drink at the bar.

The landlord, understandably taken aback at the sight of the white horse, commented, "Do you know we sell a drink named after you?"

The horse looked surprised. "What, a drink called Eric?"

A lecturer was telling his pupils what to expect of the final examination.

"It will be thirty pages long and will take more than four hours to complete the answers to the questions. Still," he added as a groan went around the room, "at least you will all be in the same boat."

"Yes," said a student, "the *Titanic!*"

63

A statistician is someone who, if he put his head in a hot oven and his feet in a bucket of ice would remark, "On average, I feel fine."

Wouldn't it be a good idea if the World Snooker Championship had five minute coughie breaks.

Teacher in classroom. "Now Tommy, who was the first man?"

"Adam," replied Tommy.

"Very good, Now who was the first woman?"

After a pause, "Madam?"

Dentist to patient: "What's your name?"
Patient: "Bacon."
Dentist: "Lean back, please!"

64

A four year old boy desperately wanted a drum for his birthday, So, the night before he prayed earnestly, "Now I lay me down to sleep, I want a drum, I pray the Lord, I want a drum, my soul to keep, and if I die before I wake, I want a drum."

A gossip gives you the benefit of the dirt.

A new music teacher at the school had formed an orchestra which was to perform at the Christmas concert. When the time came, the teacher did not feel confident that the orchestra was ready and so, on the day of the performance he whispered to each of the musicians in turn, "If you are not sure of your part, just pretend to play."

At the start of the concert he brought his baton down with a tremendous flourish and the orchestra reponded ... with a resounding silence.

Love at first sight is about as reliable as a doctor's diagnosis at first handshake.